BRINGING
CHRIST
INTO YOUR
CRISIS

How to Cope with the Coronavirus

GREG LAURIE

GOD'S ANSWER TO FEAR, WORRY AND ANXIETY

©2020 by Greg Laurie

International Standard Book Number:

978-1-61754-013-4

Printed in the United States of America

1

A STRONG HAND IN YOUR STORM

Worry. Anxiety.

It's everywhere right now, and even as you read these words, you're probably feeling it. We are hearing certain words over and over again—terms like "pandemic," "shelter in place," and "quarantine."

If you had told me just a few weeks ago that grocery stores would have empty shelves and that toilet paper would become so scarce you could almost use it as currency, I wouldn't have believed you. If you had told me that restaurants would be closing their doors, that church services would be online only, and that we wouldn't be able to meet in person, I would have said you were an alarmist—or a prepper.

And then if you would have added that it would be best for me to "self-quarantine" because I am "one of the vulnerable" to the COVID-19 virus (because I am 67), I'm afraid I would have laughed at you.

Well, it's happened. And no one is laughing now.

What a difference a few days make! The President has declared a national emergency and the United States—along with much of the rest of humanity—is in an absolute panic. Because of this unprecedented health emergency, we are now told that we have to keep our distance from one another. In some places, gatherings larger than two are now against the law. To be honest with you, I've never seen anything like this in my lifetime.

In the quiet of our enforced isolation, we find ourselves playing the "what if" game. We panic, asking ourselves, "What if this happens? What if that happens? Will there be room for me in ICU if I get sick? Will the hospital still have ventilators if I find myself unable to breathe? What about the kids? What about my elderly parents?"

These questions swirl in our minds because we have never walked through anything remotely similar to this national crisis. I am reminded of Joshua's words of caution to the Israelites as they were about to cross into Canaan: "You have not passed this way before" (Joshua 3:4, NKJV).

None of us have. This is new and frightening territory for all of us.

SO WHAT SHOULD WE DO?

First of all, we should take this crisis seriously. It isn't a bad dream or a joke or a hoax or the recap of a disaster movie. It is a real pandemic, and perhaps the worst since the Spanish Flu swept like a scythe across the globe back in 1918.

The obvious thing to do is to carefully follow the specific direction of our nation's Center for Disease Control (CDC), especially in the next few weeks. You know the drill already, don't you?

• Wash your hands.

• Practice personal distancing.

• Be selfless instead of selfish.

• Stop obsessing on non-stop newsfeeds, and think of others.

• If you are young, check in on older folks and offer them assistance.

This is a time to truly let our light shine as followers of Jesus, like a city on the hill. Helping and focusing on others can literally change your perspective of the crisis. It is well documented that volunteering elevates mood in most people—a phenomenon that has been dubbed "the helper's high."

To sum it up then, be concerned and be diligent, but don't panic. Don't allow fear, anxiety, and worry to fill your thoughts and grip your heart. In the next few pages, I wanted to share a few thoughts about that.

The word "worry" comes to us from an old English root which means "to choke." As Corrie Ten Boom once observed, "Worry does not empty tomorrow of its sorrow, it empties today of its strength. It does not enable us to escape evil, it makes us unfit to face evil when it comes. It is the interest you pay on trouble before it comes."

GOD'S PRESCRIPTION FOR WORRY

When a child is afraid of the dark, in the night, in their bedroom, the best thing to do is turn on a light in the hallway and let it stream through the open door. Then sit on the edge of the bed with that little one and speak words of comfort and reassurance. In that moment of fear or panic, they need the presence of an adult—preferably Mom or Dad—to soothe away their fears.

The same is true for us in the early hours of the morning when sleep escapes us and fear presses in from all sides. Maybe we've been watching the news or reading news sites late at night and anxious notions come sweeping into our mind, uninvited and unwelcome. In such moments, the presence of our heavenly Father can dispel all worry, fear, and anxiety.

The Lord Himself gives us these hopeful words:

> "When you pass through the waters,
> I will be with you;
> and when you pass through the rivers,
> they will not sweep over you.
> When you walk through the fire,
> you will not be burned;
> the flames will not set you ablaze."
> (Isaiah 43:2)

Know this: a son or daughter of God is indestructible until God is done with them!

In the book of Acts we encounter the story of Paul the apostle being bitten by a venomous snake, just after escaping from a shipwreck. By the way, it's a freaky thing to have a snake bite you, as I can tell you from frequent personal experience. I have been bitten by many snakes, including gopher snakes, pythons, and a boa constrictor. I had this one cranky pet python that would bite my hand every time I put it into the cage. He wouldn't bite anyone else, but he really had it out for me!

But enough about me. Scripture describes the apostle's close encounter like this: "Paul gathered a pile of brushwood and, as he put it on the fire, a viper, driven out by the heat, fastened itself on his hand.... But Paul shook the snake off into the fire and suffered no ill effects" (Acts 28:3, 5).

Vipers, of course, fall into the category of snakes you do not want to bite you. The wound from such a bite is extremely painful and can be fatal. Paul, however, calmly shook the snake off into the campfire and went on gathering wood.

Why didn't it hurt him? Why didn't the venom take his life?

Because it wasn't his time to go.

In Acts 23:11, the Lord Himself had already told Paul that he would arrive in Rome and testify before Caesar. Well then, Paul reasoned, if the Lord said he would go to Rome, he would go to Rome. Nothing could stop him. He was bulletproof. The viper bite, the hurricane, and the shipwreck were just a few inconveniences along the way. All in a day's work.

Mark 16:18 says that believers will "pick up snakes with their hands; and when they drink deadly poison, it will not hurt them at all." That doesn't mean we should be ingesting cyanide or handing rattlesnakes to each other in our church services or small groups. That would be testing God rather than trusting God, which is an evil thing. What this passage is saying, once again, is that the Christian is indestructible until God is done with them. As long as you have kingdom work to do on earth, you will remain on earth. When that work is done, He will call you home. So don't be afraid!

In the book of Genesis, God spoke to Abram and said, "Do not be afraid, Abram, for I will protect you, and your reward will be great" (Genesis 15:1, NLT). In Psalm 91, we find this promise for believers:

> You will not fear the terror of night,
> nor the arrow that flies by day,
> nor the pestilence that stalks in the darkness,
> nor the plague that destroys at midday.

A thousand may fall at your side,
ten thousand at your right hand,
but it will not come near you.
(vv. 5-7)

Isn't that great to know? It's not over until it's over! We can live our lives with boldness and an inner tranquility knowing that God is in control of everything that comes our way. Yes, we need to be wise and cautious and prudent, setting a positive example for others. But as Christians we don't have to live in constant fear for our lives because until the day we die, we will be in His protective care. And what about that day and hour when our purpose on this earth really has been fulfilled? As Paul said, "To live is Christ, and to die is gain" (Philippians 1:21). Another translation says: "Living means living for Christ, and dying is even better" (NLT). That's a great outlook to have in this dangerous, uncertain world we live in.

Right now, there is a worldwide pandemic. But let's face it, there will always be something fearful on the horizon of our lives. It goes with the territory of life on this broken planet. This coronavirus outbreak will pass, and then it will be something else. But whatever that something else might be, we can thank God that we remain under His divine protection. As with Abraham, we need to make the choice to believe His promises.

God has the answer to your fear, worry, and anxiety. We need to take the time to open His Word and listen to Him.

IN A SUDDEN STORM

In the gospel of Matthew, we have an account of Jesus and His disciples in a violent storm out on the Sea of Galilee. And that's what this current crisis is like: a vicious gale swooping down out of nowhere unlike anything we have ever witnessed or experienced before. But like every other storm, it has a beginning, a middle, and an end. Are we still in the beginning phase? Possibly. But we may also be moving toward the middle. Wherever we are in the storm, we will come through this.

Best of all, Jesus is with us. Here is Matthew's eye-witness account:

> *Immediately Jesus made the disciples get into the boat and go on ahead of him to the other side, while he dismissed the crowd. After he had dismissed them, he went up on a mountainside by himself to pray. When evening came, he was there alone, but the boat was already a considerable distance from land, buffeted by the waves because the wind was against it.*
>
> *During the fourth watch of the night Jesus went out to them, walking on the lake. When the disciples saw him walking on the lake, they were terrified. "It's a ghost," they said, and cried out in fear.*
>
> *But Jesus immediately said to them: "Take courage! It is I. Don't be afraid." (Matthew 14:22-26)*

That's a pretty good picture of where we are at right now, isn't it? In the middle of the sea. In the dark. In danger. And like the disciples, we cry out for fear. But what does Jesus reply to the men in that boat—and to us?

> *"Take courage! It is I. Don't be afraid."*

And that, of course, sets the scene for one of the most amazing accounts between the two covers of the Bible. Here is what happened next:

> *"Lord, if it's you," Peter replied, "tell me to come to you on the water."*
>
> *"Come," he said.*
>
> *Then Peter got down out of the boat, walked on the water and came toward Jesus. But when he saw the wind, he was afraid and, beginning to sink, cried out, "Lord, save me!"*
>
> *Immediately Jesus reached out his hand and caught him. "You of little faith," he said, "why did you doubt?"*
>
> *And when they climbed into the boat, the wind died down. Then those who were in the boat worshiped him, saying, "Truly you are the Son of God." (vv. 28-32)*

Let's highlight a few truths from this account that will give us courage and confidence in this storm called COVID-19.

JESUS IS WATCHING US IN OUR STORMS

Back in verse 23 we read that Jesus went up on a mountainside by Himself to pray. Mark 6:48 gives us this added detail: "He saw the disciples straining at the oars, because the wind was against them."

Out on the lake, in the boat, in the storm, the disciples were almost certainly wondering, "Where is Jesus?"

The answer is: He was watching.

He hadn't become distracted, and He wasn't an impassive observer. He was watching their every move—and I'm sure He was praying for them as well. He never lost sight of them, though He was on the mountain and they were on the sea. They may have lost sight of Him, but He never lost sight of them.

Do you feel like you are all alone in this frightening storm we are enduring, and that God has somehow lost sight of you and your needs? You aren't...and He hasn't. Nothing escapes God's attention! As Proverbs 15:3 (NKJV) tells us: "The eyes of the LORD are in every place, keeping watch on the evil and the good."

Just as surely as He was watching and praying for His followers out in that boat, He is praying and interceding for us, too. Romans 8:34 (NLT) assures us that Jesus Christ is "sitting in the place of honor at God's right hand, pleading for us." Note that this is in the present tense. It's happening right now.

So Jesus had been watching His disciples, but it didn't stop there. And what happened next would open their eyes to the power and love of Jesus as never before.

JESUS WILL COME TO US IN OUR STORMS

Matthew tells us that "Jesus went out to them, walking on the lake."

The disciples may have felt surrounded, isolated, and cut off from the Lord, but He wasn't about to let the shrieking wind or angry sea keep Him away. The most direct route to the terrified men in the boat was directly across the water, and that's the path Jesus took.

God isn't afraid of storms. In the book of Job, He spoke to his discouraged servant "out of the storm." The little book of Nahum tells us that "His way is in the whirlwind and the storm, and clouds are the dust of his feet" (1:3). When David was in serious trouble, he wrote about the Lord coming right through the storm to help him: "Mounted on a mighty angel, he sped swiftly to my aid with wings of wind. He enshrouded himself with darkness, veiling his approach with dense clouds dark as murky waters. Suddenly the brilliance of his presence broke through the clouds with lightning and a mighty storm of hail" (Psalm 18:10-12, TLB).

So Jesus was perfectly comfortable walking on the water through the darkness and the storm to rescue His men. Did you ever wonder why He didn't fly in like a helicopter? (That's what I would have done.) But that would have probably frightened them even worse. He was showing them that the very thing they fear— the wind and the sea—was only a staircase for Him to come to them in their need.

Seeing Him walk toward them across the waves, however, sent the needle on their fear meter into the red zone. They cried out, "It's a ghost!"

Why didn't the disciples recognize Jesus? They didn't recognize Him because they weren't looking for Him. Had they been waiting by faith, expecting Him to come to them, they would have recognized Him immediately. Instead, they jumped to a wildly false conclusion that this was a ghost, there to haunt them and terrify them instead of help them. Sadly, the same is sometimes true for us. We don't see the Lord in our storms because we are not actively looking for Him. But there He was, in the place they least expected Him!

You may know Jesus—perhaps you have known Him for years— but you will never know Him deeply until He comes to you in the midst of a terrible life storm. That's what Job said after all the calamity that befell him. "My ears had heard of you but now my eyes have seen you" (Job 42:5). In other words, "I have heard about how You deliver people and answer their prayers, but now I know!"

So there were the disciples, wild with fear because of the storm and the dark figure walking toward them out of the night, His robe billowing in the wind. And then a reassuring voice suddenly pierced the darkness. The Scripture says that Jesus spoke to them, saying, "Be of good cheer! It is I; do not be afraid" (Matthew 14:27, NKJV).

Can you imagine the wonder and relief that swept through that boat? They were saying, "It's Jesus! It's JESUS! We'll be all right now!" And then Peter did the impossible. He asked Jesus if he could come to Him, walking on the water as He did.

And Jesus said, "Come."

Give Peter credit. He did what no ordinary human being had ever done before. He clambered out of that boat in the middle of the sea and started walking on the water toward the Lord. Did he take tentative little baby steps, or big long strides? The Bible doesn't say. It just tells us he was out on the water, putting one foot in front of the other. But then… "when he saw the wind, he was afraid and, beginning to sink, cried out, 'Lord, save me!'" (14:30).

Does that sound familiar? Doesn't that sound just like us? We're looking to the Lord, praying, and seem to be moving along on an even keel. And then we "see the wind." We watch the latest news report. We hear the latest scary projections about COVID-19. We watch the plunging stock market numbers on the right-hand corner of the TV screen, seeing our retirement savings slip beneath the waves. And our hearts sink like a stone.

Why? Why do we get swept up in fear, anxiety, and worry? Because, like Peter, we are looking at the wind instead of looking to the Lord. Peter sank because he was afraid, and that's what makes us sink too. Fear makes us spiral down until we find ourselves drowning in our doubts. Faith gives way to fear, and trust gives way to worry. But where faith reigns—and continues to reign—fear has no place.

I once heard a doctor say, "Courage uses the same pathways as fear." So that means we have a choice, doesn't it? We can let fear and nagging worries fill the pathways of our mind, or we can allow faith to fill those same pathways with courage and hope.

WHEN WE TAKE OUR EYES OFF OF JESUS, WE BEGIN TO SINK

Up to the point where Peter got distracted by the wind and waves, he had been doing amazingly well. No other disciple had dared to do what he had done. Think about it. John wasn't out on the lake that night, testing the footing, and neither were James or Nathanael. Doubting Thomas might have been sitting in the stern, doubting whether it was a good idea. Maybe Peter's action had been an impulsive decision and maybe he hadn't thought through all the implications, but he had pushed his faith to the limit, threw his legs over the side of the boat, and started walking toward the Lord.

The first few steps were exciting, but then he took his eyes off of Jesus and put them on something else. In his case, it was the wind; in our case, it may be something else.

We start to sink when we forget about God's promises to us. We start to sink when we forget that He is in control of our lives.

But when we focus our eyes on Him, keeping the storm in our peripheral vision, we are able to walk through the darkness.

This is what kept me from sinking after our son Christopher, who was 33 years old at the time, died in a car accident back in 2008. There are no words to really describe how I felt in that moment. It seemed like my world had ended.

In contrast to the situation we are in now, we could still go out to gatherings and restaurants and be with people. And that's what we did after a few days. We got out of the house to eat together in a restaurant. But I didn't enjoy anything. Food had lost its flavor. I found myself resenting that people could laugh and have a good time and "be normal" when I was engulfed in deep pain. Everywhere we went and everything we did reminded me of Christopher.

There is only one thing that got me through. There is only one thing that kept me from floundering under those great, crashing waves of grief.

It was Jesus.

Jesus got me through. Jesus kept my head about water. It was Jesus who gripped my hand and walked me back to the boat. And it is Jesus who will get us through this storm called coronavirus. But listen... *we have to keep our eyes on Him*. If we don't, we will start to sink. Sink into depression. Sink into sadness. Sink into isolation. Sink into selfishness. Even sink into despair.

For the sake of encouragement, we need to be together in these days, reminding each other of these things. But for now, it will have to be *virtually*. Texting, calling, emailing, and posting.

Otherwise we will sink. I saw a little video last night of a family gathered outside the window of an assisted living center, singing to their 100-year-old grandmother on her birthday through the glass. We need to be communicating and reaching out to one another, making sure no one is alone, reminding each other to keep our eyes on the Lord.

Years ago in Maui, when my son Jonathan was 11 years old, I took him scuba diving with me for the first time. I am a certified, card-carrying scuba diver, but Jonathan wasn't certified yet, so we had to do an all-day training session with him.

As we were wrapping up, I said to the instructor, "Hey, when you guys go out to do a dive tomorrow, my son and I would like to go with you."

"Are you certified?" he asked me.

"Yes, I am," I replied, and casually showed him my card.

When the next day came, however, I felt queasy about it. The weather had gone south. The sky was gray, and the boats at the dock were bobbing around like crazy. My first thought was, *Man, I don't want to dive in weather like this.* I wanted to project confidence for Jonathan's sake, but it had been a long time since my last dive, and I wasn't feeling very confident, to say the least.

Out at the dive site, before we went into the water, Jonathan and I had to strap on a lot of heavy equipment. There was the inflatable vest, the scuba tanks, the regulator that you breathe through, fins, and then a weight belt around the waist. To start the dive, you have to sit on the edge of the boat with your back to the water, hold onto your mask, and fall backward.

That's the moment rookie divers dislike most—falling backward into the water with all that weight on you. And suddenly I wanted no part of it. For whatever reason, I started to panic. Falling backward into the ocean seemed like the stupidest idea I'd ever come up with. What if something went wrong? What if I couldn't get my breath? Why hadn't I been content to sit under a palm tree with a Coke and watch the waves come in? I looked over at Jonathan, and his eyes were big as saucers. If I was scared in that moment, he was terrified.

I didn't want him to see that I was frightened, too. After all, I was certified, and had a card in my wallet to prove it.

Seeing how traumatized Jonathan looked, the instructor said in a commanding voice, "Jonathan! *Look at me!*" And he waited for the eye contact. (I was looking at him, too.) Then he said, "*Remember your training.*" And Jonathan remembered, started breathing through the regulator, and over we went into the water. The truth is, everything went fine—for both of us. It's a memory I will always cherish.

That moment of focus, that moment when Jonathan heard his instructor's voice and looked into his eyes, made all the difference. It's the same for us with the storm we're in right now. Jesus is saying, "Look at Me. Don't look at the wind. Don't look at the circumstances. Don't look at the alarming reports, and don't listen to the predictions of doom. Look at Me, and remember your training. Remember the promises of God."

When we find ourselves sinking, we need to look to Jesus, and then call out to Him.

WE NEED TO CALL OUT TO JESUS

In verse 30 we read: "Beginning to sink, [Peter] cried out, 'Lord, save me!'" That has to be one of the shortest recorded prayers in the Bible. But guess what? It got through. It worked just fine. Immediately, Jesus gripped his hand, pulled him to his feet, and they walked through those surging waves together back to the boat.

Peter didn't have time to compose a long, eloquent prayer to impress the other 11 guys back in the boat. He didn't say, "Oh gracious, Lord and Savior, we come to Thee in this hour of trial, beseeching Thee for grace." He wouldn't have been able to get all of that out before his head was about six feet under water! His prayer was short, urgent, and straight from the heart.

If ever our nation was facing a wake-up call when we need to cry out to God, it is now. This isn't a time for casual prayer or flowery, poetic prayer. This is time for urgent, fervent, storm-the-gates-of-heaven prayer, that calls out to God in desperation and great urgency.

We need God in America today. We need Him to eradicate what our President has called "an invisible enemy." Scripture reminds us that "with God, all things are possible" (Matthew 19:26). In the Bible, prayer stopped storms, turned back armies, calmed waves, healed the sick, raised the dead, and in one instance, actually stopped time in its tracks (Joshua 10:12-15).

Our God has power beyond the limits of imagination and loves us more than we could fathom in a billion years. But He won't force His way into our lives. He waits for us to call on Him. He waits for us to reach out to Him and speak His name.

All across our nation and our world there are millions of nonbelievers who are gripped with fear right now. They can't go out and meet with their friends. They can't distract themselves with games or Netflix. They feel isolated and alone.

If you are one of those people, you don't have to be alone. Jesus will come into your life right now. And even though we can't assemble right now, there is a big family out there called the Church that will take you in. If you will call on the name of the Lord Jesus, He will hear you and respond.

After Peter uttered his three-word prayer, the Bible tells us that "immediately Jesus reached out his hand and caught him." I like immediately, don't you?

And no matter who you are or where you are right now, He will do the same for you. Call on Him and you will never sink. Not now, and not for eternity.

2

When Worry Comes Knocking

With our state and much of the country under a severe lockdown because of the coronavirus, I have rediscovered how much I enjoy watching birds. We have a feeder in the back yard, and living in Southern California as we do, we have quite a variety of feathered visitors who come around looking for a handout.

In His Sermon on the Mount, Jesus tells us that we can learn some important things from birds and flowers. In fact, there are important truths for us to remember in a time of national—or personal—crisis.

Here is how Jesus expressed it to a group of His followers on a sunny hillside one day.

> "That is why I tell you not to worry about everyday life—whether you have enough food and drink, or enough clothes to wear. Isn't life more than food, and your body more than clothing? Look at the birds. They don't plant or harvest or store food in barns, for your heavenly Father feeds them. And aren't you far more valuable to him than they are? Can all your worries add a single moment to your life?
>
> "And why worry about your clothing? Look at the lilies of the field and how they grow. They don't work or make their clothing, yet Solomon in all his glory was not dressed as beautifully as they are. And if God cares so wonderfully for wildflowers that are here today and thrown into the fire tomorrow, he will certainly care for you. Why do you have so little faith?

"So don't worry about these things, saying, 'What will we eat? What will we drink? What will we wear?' These things dominate the thoughts of unbelievers, but your heavenly Father already knows all your needs. Seek the Kingdom of God above all else, and live righteously, and he will give you everything you need.

"So don't worry about tomorrow, for tomorrow will bring its own worries. Today's trouble is enough for today." (Matthew 6:25-34, NLT)

THE BELIEVER SHOULD NOT WORRY

Jesus wasn't saying that a Christian shouldn't think about or be concerned with the needs of life, like what we wear or what we eat. In fact, elsewhere in Scripture we are strongly directed to work hard, save, plan for the future, exercise wisdom, and live productive, responsible lives. What Jesus is saying in this passage, however, is not to worry about these things.

In the previous pages, I pointed out that worry and anxiety can lead to deep depression—somewhere none of us wants to go. Helping others in a time of crisis, however, can lift you out of this slide into negative emotions.

With these things in mind, I thought I would provide you with a useful 10-step solution to your depression. Ready?

Step One: Do something for someone who has greater needs than you.

Step Two: repeat Step One nine more times!

Helping and focusing on others instead of yourself can literally change your mood.

In verse 25, Jesus says, "Do not worry about everyday life." The word translated into "worry" in this verse indicates something which divides, separates, or distracts us. The sense in the Greek language here is "Stop what is already being done."

In other words, stop worrying. Stop being anxious. *Stop it.*

Sometimes, however, we justify worry in our minds, almost making a virtue out of it. But worry is not a virtue. In fact, worry can actually be a sin against God. Why? Because worry reveals a lack of trust in Him. Worry indicates that we don't really believe Who He is or what He has said. Worry is never of any value in our lives. It never helps, and it always hurts.

It comes down to trusting in the providence of God. It comes down to believing that there are really no "accidents" in the life of a believer, and that nothing touches us that has not first passed through the Father's loving hands.

I'm not saying that this assurance comes easily or naturally. I've wrestled with this in my own life. But I am saying that it is absolutely essential.

In the book of Daniel, we read how the prophet, kidnapped from his homeland of Israel when he was just a teenager, faithfully and honorably served a succession of Babylonian and Persian kings.

During the reign of King Darius, Daniel was opposed by a group of Persian administrators, jealous of this Jewish man's clout in the empire. Plotting together, they came up with a scheme to have him arrested and thrown into a den of hungry lions. To his dismay,

BRINGING CHRIST INTO YOUR CRISIS

the king was trapped by a law he had ignorantly set in place, and could do nothing to save his faithful servant. Distraught and anxious, Darius spent the night worrying. Daniel, however, spending his night in the company of some suddenly tame lions, sleeping like a baby. The man who should have been awake was at rest, and the man who should have been at rest was awake.

The psalmist tells us, "God wants his loved ones to get their proper rest" (Psalm 127:2, TLB).

In Matthew 6, Jesus gives us some illustrations of why we shouldn't worry.

BIRDS DON'T WORRY, SO WHY SHOULD WE?

In verse 26 He says, "Look at the birds." In other words, look at the evidence in nature, right in front of your eyes.

Have you ever seen a stressed-out bird popping Valium? Probably not. And yet not one of the billions of birds that have lived on earth since the beginning of time has been created in the image of God as you and I have been. Birds have no hope of heaven, no prospect of eternal life, no possibility of meeting their Creator face to face, and yet every morning they get up singing!

Birds don't have to cultivate or prepare their food. It's just there for them every day because the Father sets the table. Some eat insects, some eat vegetation, and of course there are some in the McDonald's parking lot that have developed a taste for French fries.

Have you ever heard this old Elizabeth Cheney poem about birds?

Said the robin to the sparrow, "I should really like to know,
Why these anxious human beings rush about and hurry so."
Said the sparrow to the robin, "Friend, I think that it must be,
That they have no heavenly Father such as cares for you and me."

Jesus was pretty pointed when He drew His conclusion about birds. He said, "And aren't you far more valuable to him than they are? Can all your worries add a single moment to your life?" So, if God takes thought for each and every bird and provides food for all of them. Don't you imagine that He is also thinking about you, and will provide for your needs, too?

Moving on from the birds in the sky, Jesus must have gestured to the grassy hillside, drawing the attention of His disciples to the little wild lilies growing there.

FLOWERS DON'T WORRY, SO WHY SHOULD WE?

"And why worry about your clothing? Look at the lilies of
the field and how they grow. They don't work or make their
clothing, yet Solomon in all his glory was not dressed as
beautifully as they are." (vv. 28-29)

Jesus did a lot of His teaching out of doors. He used the sky and clouds, vineyards and fruit trees, wind and rain, hens and chicks, fish and streams, sunrises and sunsets, and rocks and rainbows to illustrate spiritual truths. All of nature was His blackboard. And who better to teach that way than the Creator of all?

Probably gesturing to the humble wildflowers around him, He was saying, "Check out these little flowers. Have you ever taken time to look at a single blossom up close? Even Solomon dressed in his royal robes in his lavish palace overlaid with silver, gold, and ivory didn't have the beauty of these wildflowers of Galilee."

Think about how people obsess about their appearance and their wardrobe. It was said that Imelda Marcos, widow of the late Philippines strong man Ferdinand Marcos, had over 3,000 pairs of shoes in a walk-in closet that was probably bigger than my whole house. If television commercials are any guide, people also obsess about their bodies and how they appear to other people.

That's understandable, of course. We all want to look good. We want to present ourselves well. In fact, some people ought to care more! But it crosses the line when we are completely preoccupied by these things to the point that we neglect our spiritual life and our relationship with God.

Flowers, lovely as they may be, fade quickly. Some flowers, like day lilies, bloom for just one day, and then quickly wither. Our bodies are also "temporary housing," and not meant to last very long. The apostles Paul and Peter called their bodies "tents," but they knew that the spiritual part of us will still be alive a million years from now.

Again, Jesus made the point that if God takes such care to clothe the common little wildflowers with beauty, He will surely take care of His sons and daughters who will live forever.

WORRY DOESN'T MAKE LIFE LONGER, IT JUST MAKES IT MORE MISERABLE

Worry doesn't resolve problems; it just creates new ones.

In verse 27, Jesus asked this pointed question: "Can all your worries add a single moment to your life?"

The answer, of course, is no. You can't lengthen your life by thinking and worrying about the length of your life! In fact, your stress and high blood pressure might shorten it—or at least make it more miserable. Length of life is determined by God, not by us. The Bible says of King David, "For when David had served God's purpose in his own generation, he fell asleep; he was buried with his fathers" (Acts 13:36).

The best we can hope for in this life is to serve God's purposes; it's up to Him how long that service will be. Life is a gift from God, and each new day is a fresh opportunity to make ourselves available to Him. In Psalm 90:9 (KJV), Moses says that "we spend our years as a tale that is told." And whether that tale is brief or long—a short story or a novel—all of its pages belong to Him.

In verse 36 Jesus says, "If God cares so wonderfully for wildflowers that are here today and thrown into the fire tomorrow, he will certainly care for you. Why do you have so little faith?"

He didn't say, "You have no faith"; He said, "You have *little* faith."

That's the way it is with many of us. Because of their weak or "little faith," some are more prone to worry and anxiety through the course of their lives. It actually shapes their personality. It seems like they are always worried, stressed, afraid, or defeated. They are mastered by their circumstances, instead of mastering them. They believe in Jesus for salvation, but have a difficult time believing Him in the crush of daily needs and circumstances. When something hard comes their way, a test or a challenge, they are bowled over by it.

The coronavirus is a test. A national test. A global test. Perhaps the greatest test of our times. The government orders to "shelter in place" are concerning to everyone, but to some people, they are a nightmare. Their fear is off the charts. This should not be true for those who have placed their lives in God's hands for safekeeping.

Psalm 27:5 says, "For in the day of trouble he will keep me safe in his dwelling; he will hide me in the shelter of his tabernacle and set me high upon a rock."

AN OPPORTUNITY TO GROW IN THE WORD

I often hear people say, "I'm too busy to read the Bible. I just can't seem to find the time."

Well, there's time now!

I highly recommend getting into your Bible as an alternative to watching nonstop cable news programs with their cynical commentators or binging on endless Netflix movies. If we seize the opportunity before us, God can use this unprecedented event in our nation's history to make us spiritually stronger.

So how do we grow in faith?

By reading, studying, believing, and memorizing God's Word.

Yes, I know that we have to keep up with the news and stay aware of changing situations in the world as the pandemic spreads. But you won't find any lasting comfort there. You won't find courage and strength and wisdom and overcoming hope. You'll only find those in the Word of God. And yes, watching movies on TV is a distraction from reality—and we need that now and then. But you won't find any guidance or direction for life in times of great crisis coming out of Hollywood studios. Only God's Word has the truth you need to navigate in perilous times. The psalmist said, "Your word is a lamp to my feet and a light to my path" (Psalm 119:105).

In Romans 10:17 (NKJV), Paul writes: "So then faith comes by hearing, and hearing by the word of God." When we open our eyes and ears to the Word of God, it puts everything in perspective. With the help of God's Spirit, you find yourself able to function and make productive choices—even in chaotic moments like these. The fact is, most Americans own Bibles, but few actually read them. Surveys show that the average American household has at least four Bibles—mostly collecting dust.

The Center for Bible Engagement released an eye-opening study on the power of regular Bible reading. The researchers discovered that if you aren't reading your Bible four or more times a week, you will make no significant choices or changes that are any different from someone who doesn't read the Bible at all. However, if you do get into God's Word more than four times a week, you can expect results like these:

- Your propensity for pornography goes down 61 percent.

- Your propensity for gambling falls by 74 percent.

- Your propensity for obesity falls by 20 percent.

Again, If you read your Bible at least four days a week:

- You have a 228 percent greater chance of sharing your faith.

- You have a 231 percent greater chance of discipling others.

- You have a 407 percent chance of memorizing Scripture.

Reading your Bible at least four times a week will literally change your life. Why? Because the Bible is like no other book on earth. Its pages are literally alive with truth. Hebrews 4:12 (TLB) tells us that "whatever God says to us is full of living power: it is sharper than the sharpest dagger, cutting swift and deep into our innermost thoughts and desires with all their parts, exposing us for what we really are."

TRADE YOUR WORRY FOR WORSHIP

Instead of worrying, put God and His Word first in your life. Here is how Jesus expressed it:

> "So do not worry, saying, 'What shall we eat?' or 'What shall we drink?' or 'What shall we wear?' For the pagans run after all these things, and your heavenly Father knows that you need them. But seek first his kingdom and his righteousness, and all these things will be given to you as well." (Matthew 6:31-33)

Rather than obsessing about food, drink, or clothing like unbelievers do, Jesus tells us to focus our attention and hopes on things of the Lord. As we do this, God will take care of all our needs.

At this moment of national crisis, many of us have found ourselves very concerned about our investments, our employment, and our future. We wonder how we will get by if the economy crashes or our country teeters into a deep recession. These is nothing wrong with these sorts of concerns. But Jesus isn't saying, "Stick your head in the sand," or "Don't be concerned." He is saying, "Don't worry about these things. Don't let anxiety consume you."

There is something about putting God first—first in our thoughts, first in our plans, and first in our hopes. Giving Him the first few minutes of every day to read His Word and seek His face in prayer. When we do that, the rest of life seems to fall into place.

What does Matthew 6:33 mean when it says to seek Him first? Think about it like this. If you lost a two-carat diamond ring somewhere in your house, you would turn the place upside down until you found it. You wouldn't be half-hearted or casual about it. You wouldn't say, "Well, I'll look for it later tonight—after supper and after I watch *Jeopardy.*"

To "seek first" means to give that search priority above everything else. What then does it mean to seek "the kingdom of God"? It means that we prioritize *the rule and reign of Jesus Christ in our lives.*

In the Lord's prayer, Jesus taught us to pray, "Your kingdom come, Your will be done." But we can't pray "Your kingdom" until we first pray "my kingdom go!" When I put God and His kingdom first, my life will find its proper balance.

In verse 33, the Lord promises that when we do this, when we put Him first, then "all these things will be added unto you." What things does He mean? He's talking about what we will eat, drink and wear, where we will live and work, and whom we will marry. He is saying that God will take care of the basic issues of our lives when we consciously prioritize our relationship with Him and put Him first.

The next time you feel worry knocking on the door of your thoughts, send Jesus to the door to meet it.

TURN YOUR PANIC INTO PRAYER

If you don't want to live in anxiety, fear, and worry, put that troubling issue—whatever it is—in God's hands. In Philippians 4:6, the apostle Paul gave us a potent, succinct plan for defeating the negative emotions that assail us:

*Do not be anxious about anything, but in everything,
by prayer and petition, with thanksgiving, present your
requests to God. And the peace of God, which transcends
all understanding, will guard your hearts and your minds in
Christ Jesus.*

One of my friends tried to keep in touch with his elderly mother-in-law who was spending her last days in a care center. Every time he called to encourage her, however, she would turn the tables by quoting this verse to him from her King James Bible: "Be anxious for NOTHING," she would say, emphasizing the word "nothing." And the Lord used that verse, and the promise that He would stand guard over her heart and mind, to ease her way into His presence.

As someone has wisely said, "When your knees start knocking, kneel on them!" Often when we face adversity our first instinct it to turn to people for help—to pick up the phone and connect with someone we know and love. Reaching out like that is usually a good idea, especially in a deep crisis. But before you pick up the phone to call someone or send a text, try this:

Turn to the Lord first.

Talk to Him before you speak to anyone else.

Ask Him before you question anyone else.

Cry out to Him before you punch in those familiar phone numbers. Then, when you do make that call, you will be in a better place with a better perspective. You will be prepared to help someone, instead of just unloading on someone.

We must teach ourselves to turn to God.

"WITH THANKSGIVING..."

"...But in everything, by prayer and petition, with thanksgiving...."

Most of us are in tune with the concept of offering thanks to God after He has heard our cry for help and answered our prayers. But this is thanksgiving before the prayer is answered. This is thanking and praising God in the very midst of calling out to Him for help. And because I take time to worship my Father and remind myself of His greatness and power, by so doing I automatically put my own problems and issues into their proper perspective.

Looping back to the story of Daniel for a moment, when he heard about the new government edict outlawing prayers to God—on the pain of death—Scripture tells us how he responded. It says, "When Daniel learned that the law had been signed, he went home and knelt down as usual in his upstairs room, with its windows open toward Jerusalem. He prayed three times a day, just as he had always done, giving thanks to his God" (Daniel 6:10, NLT)

What he did was an incredible act of courage, but don't miss the substance of his prayer. He poured out thanks to God! In spite of his situation, which anyone would describe as desperate, he filled His prayer with praise, worship, and thanksgiving. (I might have been praying, "Lord, zap those evil people who hate me!")

REPLACE ANXIOUS THOUGHTS WITH BETTER ONES

A little further on in Philippians 4, we come across these strong words:

Finally, brothers, whatever is true, whatever is noble, whatever is right, whatever is pure, whatever is lovely, whatever is admirable—if anything is excellent or praiseworthy—think about such things.

Maintaining personal peace involves both the heart and the mind. Isaiah 26:3 (NKJV) says, "You will keep him in perfect peace, whose mind is stayed on You, because he trusts in You."

Why do our thoughts matter? Because what we think about ultimately affects what we do. Solomon wrote, "For as [a man] thinks within himself, so he is" (Proverbs 23:7, NASB). In 2 Corinthians 10:5, Paul tells us that we actually have the capacity to "take captive every thought to make it obedient to Christ."

Remind yourself of these things, especially in this worldwide pandemic crisis. The next time you find yourself slipping into worry, try talking some sense to yourself! We need to train our minds to think biblically. and to rein in our runaway emotions. Faith, as wonderful as it is, doesn't kick in automatically. We have to apply it. We have to deliberately step out into it.

Over in Psalm 42 we read that the psalmist was deeply troubled and depressed. He felt himself sinking, losing control to his emotions. In the midst of it, he suddenly cried out with these words:

Why are you downcast, O my soul?
Why so disturbed within me?
Put your hope in God,
for I will yet praise him,
my Savior and my God.
(vv. 5-6)

He talked to himself! In other words, he applied faith, reason, and biblical thinking to the situation. He grabbed himself by the scruff of the neck, gave himself a little shake, and said, "Hope in God!" And it worked.

Every believer needs to do this, regardless of how long he or she has known the Lord. Even if you have walked with God since you were a little child, you can still have a lapse of faith and experience a moment of despair. You can find yourself in a time where you can't see beyond your pain and don't understand what's going on in your life. It happens to the best of us, just as it happened to the psalmist. The next time you find yourself struggling with fear over the COVID-19 virus—or any other frightening situation in life—talk to yourself. Quote Scripture to yourself. Remind yourself of what is true and what will always be true.

FOR BELIEVERS ONLY

Let me say one last thing about these wonderful promises we have been talking about in these pages. They are for believers only. To experience God's tender care and companionship in these difficult days, you must be born again. If you are His child, He promises to watch over you. He promises eternal life beyond the grave.

But if you don't know the Lord, these promises don't apply. And quite frankly, you should worry. Jesus told us to "seek first His kingdom," but before you can do that you have to be born again. You have to know Him as Savior and Lord. Facing this huge worldwide crisis as we are, you may realize that it's time to make a change in your life.

But you can't do it by yourself.

You need to come to Jesus.

In Matthew 11:28 (NLT), He was speaking to every one of us when He said, "Come to me, all of you who are weary and carry heavy burdens, and I will give you rest."

If you want the Lord to intervene in your life as you face storms, He will be there for you. He will immediately reach out to grasp your hand in your hour of need, just as He reached out and took hold of Peter.

Remember what He said in that moment? "O you of little faith, why did you doubt?" (Matthew 11:31, NKJV). The words "little faith" is one word in the original Greek. *Littlefaith*. It's almost like a nickname. There is tenderness in it. It's as though Jesus is gently shaking His head and saying, "Oh Littlefaith. You were doing so well. Making real strides. What happened?"

But guess what happened next. Littlefaith Peter got his eyes back on Jesus and walked on water again back to the boat!

Maybe you're in one of those moments—out in the middle of the sea and beginning to sink. You might be in the grip of some addiction. Your marriage might be in trouble. Maybe you or someone you love has been tested positive for coronavirus, and you find yourself quarantined with fear.

Follow Littlefaith's example and cry out, "Lord, save me!" He won't rebuke or turn away a person who is trying to come to Him by faith.

This crisis we are in may not be resolved in three weeks or three months. The storm may rage on for a while. But here's the truth:

It is safer to be with Jesus on the water in the storm than to be without Him in the boat.

WHY IS THIS HAPPENING TO ME?

There are two verses in Romans chapter 8 that have encouraged believers for thousands of years. Most of us are familiar with Romans 8:28: "And we know that in all things God works for the good of those who love him, who have been called according to his purpose." But after verse 28 comes verse 29—and it's every bit as magnificent: "For those God foreknew he also predestined to be conformed to the likeness of his Son."

So what is Paul saying here? Whatever happens in your life will always work for your good if it makes you more like Jesus. Although you and I are often caught up with what is temporarily good, God is interested in what is eternally good. He is looking at the long term, to make us more like the Lord Jesus Himself.

I love the story that Chuck Swindoll tells in his book, *Esther, a Woman of Strength and Dignity*. Let me retell it here in brief. Chuck writes about a man who had been shipwrecked on an uninhabited island. Over the next number of days, in the hours he could spare from hunting for food, he painstakingly built himself a little hut to shelter from the elements. He also used the hut to protect the few precious items he had been able to salvage from the shipwreck that had stranded him there.

For weeks, he lived in this little hut, enduring the hot days and cold nights as best he could. Every day he scanned the horizon, praying for the approach of a ship. But none came.

Then one evening, when he returned from his search for food, he was horrified to see his little hut in flames. He tried to put out the fire, but it was too late. Everything he had in his world had gone up in smoke.

He went to sleep that night, listening to the pounding of the surf, stunned and depressed at his misfortune. The next morning, however, his sorrow turned to delight when he saw a ship anchored off the island—the first ship he had seen in all the weeks he had been marooned. Still trying to believe his eyes, he heard footsteps, and then looked up to see the ship's captain approaching him.

"We saw your smoke signal," the captain said, "and came to rescue you."

The point of the story is clear. What may seem like a disaster today might be a smoke signal, leading to an unexpected and life-changing deliverance.

As I write these words, our nation is in the jaws of a frightening pandemic, unlike anything we have faced in living memory. Nearly everyone in our country has been or will be impacted by this crisis. And what will our response be?

Will men and women rethink the priorities of their lives, and turn to God for help?

Will America repent and turn from sin and arrogant self-sufficiency?

Will the powerful, saving name of Jesus Christ be lifted up across our land?

Will families forced to "shelter in place" under one roof learn to value one another as never before?

If a national disaster softens hearts toward God and leads to the eternal salvation of many in America and around the world, we may one day look back on it as a "severe mercy."

The prophet Jeremiah assures us with these words about God:

> *If he works severely, he also works tenderly.*
> *His stockpiles of loyal love are immense.*
> *He takes no pleasure in making life hard,*
> *in throwing roadblocks in the way.*
> *(Lamentations 3:32–33, MESSAGE)*

God wants what is best for each one of us.

And what is best is always a closer relationship with Jesus Christ.

3

America, It's Time to Pray!

You can see it on people's faces. They are frightened, alarmed, and feel as though they don't have control.

And they are right. They don't have control. None of us do.

It's time to pray as never before. We need God in America today. We need the Lord to step in and turn back this virus. It's time to turn our panic into prayer, because the sources that we usually turn to for comfort can't do anything for us.

Hollywood can't save us. There is no blockbuster film or actor that will get us out of this.

The media can't save us. They are as confused and frightened as any of us, and have difficulty separating truth from rumor and error.

Technology can't save us. Our latest versions of the iPhone or Android honestly just feed us with more real-time information to stoke our stress and amplify our anxiety.

Washington DC can't save us from this pandemic. Our leaders will (hopefully) work together and do what they can, but this is beyond them. Even the President of the United States can't get us out of this. He has put together an excellent task force to deal with the coronavirus, but they can't fix this for us, though we should take their advice seriously.

That is why the President wisely called for a National Day of Prayer. In his proclamation, he stated: "As your President, I ask you to pray for the health and well-being of your fellow Americans and to remember that no problem is too big for God to handle. We should all take to heart the holy words found in 1 Peter 5:7: 'Casting all your care upon him, for he careth for you.' Let us pray that all those affected by the virus will feel the presence of our Lord's protection and love during this time. With God's help, we will overcome this threat."

We need to keep praying, because the worst of this virus may still be coming. But you need to know this: God is bigger than the coronavirus—or any virus. He is bigger than any problem you may be facing right now, no matter how complex or unsolvable it may seem to you.

James 4:2 says, "You do not have, because you do not ask God." And the Lord promises, "Call to Me, and I will answer you, and show you great and mighty things, which you do not know" (Jeremiah 33:3, NKJV).

Yes, it's time to pray.

There was a godly king in the Bible, named Jehoshaphat, who found himself in big trouble. Word came to him that their strong, well-equipped armies were marching toward Jerusalem, bent on destroying the King of Judah and his people. The attack was unprovoked and a complete surprise. There was no time to organize defenses, build new walls, or send out peace proposals. Complete disaster had arrived on their very doorstep.

Terrified, Jehoshaphat quickly gathered the nation and asked everyone—men, women, and even little ones—to fast and pray. He cried out to God with these words: "O our God, won't you stop them? We are powerless against this mighty army that is about to attack us. We do not know what to do, but we are looking to you for help" (2 Chronicles 20:12, NLT).

And guess what happened? God answered their prayer as the enemy armies suddenly and inexplicably turned on one another and utterly destroyed themselves.

The fact is, there is a spiritual element to every problem you and I will face in our lives. And this is a time to pray.

Here is a promise from God: "If I ever shut off the supply of rain from the skies or order the locusts to eat the crops or send a plague on my people, and my people, my God-defined people, respond by humbling themselves, praying, seeking my presence, and turning their backs on their wicked lives, I'll be there ready for you: I'll listen from heaven, forgive their sins, and restore their land to health" (2 Chronicles 7:14, MESSAGE).

God says we need to humble ourselves, pray, seek His presence, and turn our backs on our sin and our selfish ways. If we do that, the Lord promises to hear our prayers, forgive our sins and restore our land to health.

God keeps His promises.

Let's be praying.

ONE FINAL THOUGHT-

The most important prayer you can pray right now if you are not yet a Christian is something along the lines of:

"God, I am sorry for my sin.

I turn from it now.

Thank you for sending your son, Jesus Christ to die on the cross for my sin.

I ask Him to come into my life right now.

I choose to follow Him from this day forward.

In Jesus name I pray, amen."

If you prayed that prayer, I would love to hear from you.

I will send you a free Bible in the mail that is called "The New Believer's Bible".

It is the New Living Translation accompanied by hundreds of notes that I wrote to encourage you in your new relationship with God.

---

[1] http://www.abrahamlincolnonline.org/lincoln/speeches/fast.htm
[2] Source: https://www.centerforbibleengagement.org/
[3] Retold from an illustration; Charles Swindoll, Esther: A Woman of Strength and Dignity (Nashville, Tennessee: Word Publishing, Inc., 1997)
[4] The title of a book by Sheldon Vanauken

PASTOR GREG'S DAILY DEVOTIONS

GET CONNECTED TODAY!

Sign up today for Greg Laurie's email devotions. You'll receive daily encouragement and relevant teaching in a quick, bite-sized format during the week.

TO GET GREG'S DAILY DEVOTIONS

visit: harvest.org

Get more resources to help you grow in your faith at store.harvest.org.

ONLINE TRAINING COURSES

TELL SOMEONE

Get equipped to confidently share your faith in Christ with boldness and tact. This free online course will help you use your personal testimony to build a bridge and bring the Good News of Jesus to those around you.

WHAT EVERY GROWING CHRISTIAN NEEDS TO KNOW

As believers, it is important that we grow in our relationship with Jesus Christ. We all should have a desire to be mature, growing Christians. There are key disciplines that we must follow in order to effectively grow, and Harvest wants to help you understand and establish those habits.

NEW BELIEVER'S ONLINE COURSE

It's important to get off on the right foot in our walk with Christ. And to do that, we must develop good spiritual habits, like reading God's Word and praying daily, attending church regularly, and sharing our faith. In this course, Pastor Jonathan Laurie takes us through the four steps that every new believer needs to take in order to become a strong, mature follower of Jesus.

HAPPINESS ONLINE COURSE

People chase after many things trying to find happiness, things like fame, wealth, and pleasure. But in the end, those things only leave a feeling of emptiness and misery. According to Scripture, the only place to find true happiness is in a relationship with God. In this course, Pastor Greg shows us how to find that true happiness by following Jesus and loving others.

GET STARTED AT:
COURSES.HARVEST.ORG

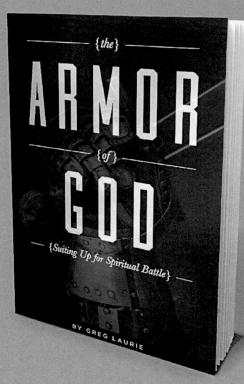

FREE EBOOK

THE ARMOR OF GOD: SUITING UP FOR SPIRITUAL BATTLE

Have you ever been humming along nicely as a Christian, when suddenly you were barraged with all kinds of temptations and attacks, trials and difficulties?

Ephesians 6:10–18 tells us to put on the full armor of God. We must remind ourselves daily to put on our entire armor, so we will not be vulnerable in any area of life. Enjoy this free ebook to equip you for spiritual attacks and temptations.

VISIT:
HTTPS://HARVEST.ORG/RESOURCES/EBOOKS/

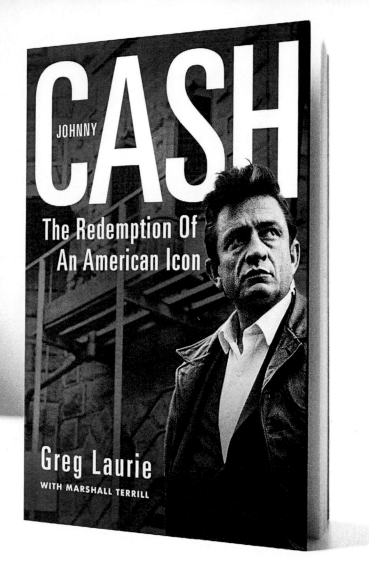

Johnny Cash: The Redemption of an American Icon
dives deep into the singer's inner demons, triumphs, and gradual return to faith. Laurie interviews Cash's family, friends, and business associates to reveal how the singer's true success came through finding the only Person whose star was bigger than his own.

**GET YOUR COPY TODAY!
STORE.HARVEST.ORG**

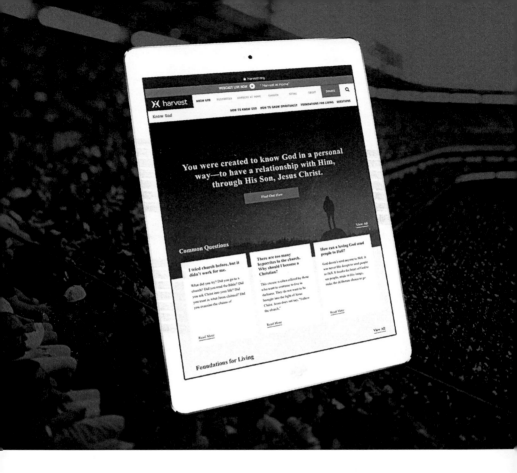

"You were created to know God in a personal way—to have a relationship with Him, through His Son, Jesus Christ."

FIND OUT MORE:
HTTPS://HARVEST.ORG/KNOW-GOD/

"Get the latest news from Pastor Greg, with weekly articles that touch on faith and culture. Pastor Greg provides biblical insight to current events. "

SEE MORE:
HTTPS://HARVEST.ORG/RESOURCES/GREGS-BLOG/

Greg Laurie
Podcast

Greg Laurie delivers compelling, practical insights on faith, culture, and current events—with an emphasis on the saving power of the gospel message. Subscribe to daily programming from A New Beginning, special messages, and exclusive interviews—all on the Greg Laurie Podcast.

LISTEN ON APPLE PODCASTS, SPOTIFY, AND MORE!